KEN FOLLETT

NOTRE-DAME

At least 50p per copy on each sale of this book will go to
the charity La Fondation du Patrimoine

MACMILLAN

First published 2019 in France by Éditions Robert Laffont

First published in the UK 2019 by Macmillan
an imprint of Pan Macmillan
The Smithson, 6 Briset Street, London EC1M 5NR
Associated companies throughout the world
www.panmacmillan.com

ISBN 978-1-5290-3764-7

1 3 5 7 9 8 6 4 2

A CIP catalogue record for this book is available from the British Library.

Typeset by Palimpsest Book Production Ltd, Falkirk, Stirlingshire
Printed and bound by CPI Group (UK) Ltd, Croydon, CR0 4YY

Visit **www.panmacmillan.com** to read more about all our books
and to buy them. You will also find features, author interviews and
news of any author events, and you can sign up for e-newsletters
so that you're always first to hear about our new releases.

It was one of those spring days that are so gentle and pretty that all Paris treats them like Sundays, crowding the squares and the boulevards. During such days of clear skies, warmth and peace, there comes a supreme moment at which to appreciate the portal of Notre-Dame. It is when the sun, already sinking, shines almost directly on the cathedral. Its rays, more and more horizontal, slowly leave the pavement and climb the vertical façade to highlight the countless carvings against their shadows, until the great rose window, like the eye of a cyclops, is reddened as if by reflections from a furnace.

Victor Hugo, *The Hunchback of Notre-Dame*

Today, they weep for her in every language.

Paris Match

I

2019

The voice on the phone was urgent. 'I'm in Paris,' it said. 'Turn on your television!'

I was at home, in the kitchen, with Barbara, my wife. We had just finished supper. I had not drunk any wine, which turned out to be a good thing. I did not yet know it, but the evening was going to be a long one.

The voice on the phone belonged to an old friend. She has weathered many crises as a Member of Parliament and a Cabinet minister, and is completely unflappable, but she sounded shocked.

You know what we saw on the screen: the wonderful Cathedral of Notre-Dame de Paris, one of the greatest achievements of European civilization, was on fire.

The sight dazed and disturbed us profoundly. I was on the edge of tears. Something priceless was dying in front of our eyes. The feeling was bewildering, as if the earth was shaking.

I know the building well. One Christmas Barbara and I went to midnight Mass there. Thousands of people thronged the church. The dim lights cast deep shadows in the aisles, the carols echoed in the nave, and the vault high above us was cloaked in darkness. Most moving of all was the knowledge that our ancestors had been celebrating Christmas this way in this building for more than eight hundred years.

I had visited the church many other times. My earliest sight of it had been in 1966, on my first holiday outside the UK, although at the age of seventeen I'm afraid I was too interested in the girls in our group to pay serious attention to a cathedral. My last had been only four weeks earlier, when I had driven along the Left Bank and, as always, had drunk in the magnificent view of the twin towers and the flying buttresses.

As soon as I began to think rationally about what I was seeing on television, I understood what was burning and how the fire was gathering force, but the journalists commenting did not – and why should they? They had not studied the construction of Gothic cathedrals. I had, in doing research for *The Pillars of the Earth*, my novel about the building of a fictional medieval cathedral. A key scene in Chapter Four describes the old cathedral of Kingsbridge burning down, and I had asked myself: Exactly how does a great stone church catch fire?

I had climbed up into the dusty spaces under the roofs of cathedrals including Canterbury and Florence. I had stood on the mighty beams that spanned the naves and looked up at the rafters that supported the leads. I had noticed the dried-up debris that often gathers in such places: old bits of wood and rope, sandwich wrappers left by maintenance workers, the knitted twigs of birds' nests and the papery homes of wasps. I felt sure that the Notre-Dame fire had started somewhere in the roof, probably when a dropped cigarette or a spark from an electrical fault ignited some litter, which in turn had set the timbers ablaze. And the damage resulting from that threatened to flatten the building.

I decided to share this thought with others, so I tweeted:

The rafters consist of hundreds of tonnes of wood, old and very dry. When that burns the roof collapses, then the falling debris destroys the vaulted ceiling, which also falls and destroys the mighty stone pillars that are holding the whole thing up.

That turned out to be about right, except that I underestimated the strength of the pillars and the vaults, both of which were damaged but, happily, not completely obliterated.

Here's how the destruction of Kingsbridge Cathedral happened in *Pillars*, seen from the point of view of Prior Philip:

A crashing sound made him look up. Immediately above him, an enormous timber was moving slowly sideways. It was going to fall on top of him. He dashed back into the south transept, where Cuthbert stood looking scared.

A whole section of the roof, three triangles of beam-and-rafter plus the lead sheets nailed to them, was falling in. Philip and Cuthbert watched, transfixed, quite forgetting their own safety. The roof fell on one of the big round arches of the crossing. The enormous weight of the falling wood and lead cracked the stonework of the arch with a prolonged explosive sound like thunder. Everything happened slowly: the beams fell slowly, the arch broke up slowly, and the smashed masonry fell slowly through the air. More roof beams came free, and then, with a noise like a long slow peal of thunder, a whole section of the north wall of the chancel shuddered and slid sideways into the north transept.

Philip was appalled. The sight of such a mighty building being destroyed was strangely shocking. It was like watching a mountain fall down or a river run dry: he had never really thought it could happen. He could hardly believe his eyes.

As night fell on 15 April 2019, the people of Paris came out into the streets, and the television cameras showed thousands of grief-stricken faces lit by the flames, some singing hymns, others just weeping as they watched their beloved cathedral burn. The tweet that got the most heartfelt response from my followers that night just said:

Francais, francaises, nous partagons votre tristesse.
Frenchmen, Frenchwomen, we share your sadness.

It should have been *nous partageons* with an 'e', but no one minded.

There are people who understand more about medieval cathedrals than I do, but the journalists don't know their names. They know mine because of my books, and they know that *Pillars* is about a cathedral, so within a few minutes I started to get messages from the newsrooms. I spent that evening doing television, radio and press interviews, explaining in English and French what was happening on the Île de la Cité.

At the same time as giving interviews, I was watching.

The central spire, slender as an arrowhead and three hundred feet high, was a possible starting-point of the fire, and now it was blazing infernally. It was made of 500 tonnes of oak beams with a lead roof weighing 250 tonnes, and the burning wood rapidly became too weak to support the burden of all that lead. The most heart-stopping moment of the evening, for the grieving crowds on the streets and the horrified millions watching television, came when the spire leaned sideways, snapped like a matchstick, and crashed through the flaming roof of the nave.

Notre-Dame had always seemed eternal, and the medieval builders certainly thought it would last until the Day of Judgement; but suddenly we saw that it could be destroyed. In the life of every boy there is a painful moment when he realizes that his father is not all-powerful and invulnerable. The old man has weaknesses, he may become ill, and one day he will die. The fall of the spire made me think of that moment.

It seemed that the nave was already a ruin. I thought I saw flames in one of the two towers, and I knew that if they fell the entire church would be destroyed.

President Emmanuel Macron, a radical modernizing leader who was in the middle of a bitter and violent battle with those who disliked his reforms, spoke to the cameras and became, for a time at least, the recognized leader of a united French nation. He impressed the world, and he brought tears to this Welshman's eyes when he said with firm confidence: 'Nous rebâtirons.' 'We will rebuild.'

At midnight I went to bed and set my alarm clock

for 4.30 a.m., as my last phone call had been a request to appear on breakfast television early the following day.

I feared that the sun would rise on a smoking pile of rubble in the Île de la Cité where Notre-Dame had so proudly stood. I was immensely heartened to see most of the walls still standing, as well as the great pair of square towers at the west end. It was not as bad as everyone had feared, and I drove to the television studio with a message of hope.

I spent Tuesday doing interviews, then on Wednesday I flew to Paris for a discussion on the TV programme *La Grande Librairie* (*The Big Bookstore*) about the symbolism of cathedrals in literature and in life.

It never occurred to me to stay at home. Notre-Dame is too close to my heart. I'm not a religious believer, yet despite that I go to church. I love the architecture, the music, the words of the Bible and the sense of sharing something profound with other people. I have long found deep spiritual peace in the great cathedrals, as do many millions of people, believers and non-believers alike. And I have another reason to feel grateful for the cathedrals: my love of them inspired the novel that is certainly my most popular book and probably my best.

President Macron said Notre-Dame would be rebuilt in five years. One of the French newspapers responded with a headline that translates: 'Macron believes in miracles.' But French attachment to Notre-Dame is profound. It has been the stage for some of the key events in French history. Every road sign that tells you how far you are from Paris measures the distance to Kilometre Zero, a bronze star embedded in

The author (right) speaking with Philippe Villeneuve,
chief architect of the reconstruction of Notre-Dame

the pavement in front of Notre-Dame. The great bell called Emmanuel, in the south tower, can be heard all over the city when it rings its deep F sharp for joy or sorrow, the end of war or a tragedy such as 9/11.

Besides, it is always unwise to underestimate the French. If anyone can do it, they can.

Before I flew home from Paris, my French publisher asked me if I would think about writing something new about my love of Notre-Dame, in light of the terrible event of 15 April. Profits from the book would go to the rebuilding fund, and so would my royalties. 'Yes,' I said. 'I'll start tomorrow.'

This is what I wrote.

2

1163

Maurice de Sully, bishop of Paris

The Cathedral of Notre-Dame was too small in 1163. The population of Paris was growing. On the right bank of the river, commerce was surging to levels unknown in the rest of medieval Europe, and on the left bank the university was attracting students from many countries. Between the two, on an island in the river, stood the cathedral, and Bishop Maurice de Sully felt it should be bigger.

And there was something else. The existing building was in the round-arched style we call Romanesque, but there was an exciting new architectural movement that used pointed arches, letting more light into the building, a look now called Gothic. This style had been pioneered only six miles from Notre-Dame, at the abbey church of Saint-Denis – burial place of the French kings – which had brilliantly combined several technical and visual innovations: as well as the pointed arch, it featured piers of clustered shafts sprouting ribs up into a high vault that was lighter in weight; a semicircular walkway at the east end to keep pilgrims moving past the relics of Saint Denis; and, outside, graceful flying buttresses that facilitated larger windows and made the massive church look as if it were about to take flight.

Maurice must have seen the new church of Saint-Denis and become enamoured of it. No doubt it made Notre-Dame look old-fashioned. Perhaps he was even a little jealous of Abbot Suger at Saint-Denis, who had encouraged two successive master-masons to experiment boldly, with triumphantly successful results. So Maurice ordered his cathedral to be knocked down and replaced by a Gothic church.

Let me pause. All the above sounds straightforward, but in fact it is astonishing. The Cathedral of Notre-Dame de Paris, along with most of the great Gothic churches that are still the most beautiful buildings in the cities of Europe, was erected in the Middle Ages, a time marked by violence, famine and plague.

The construction of a cathedral was a huge enterprise lasting decades. Chartres Cathedral was built in twenty-six years, and Salisbury in thirty-eight years, but they were unusually quick. Notre-Dame de Paris took almost one hundred years, and improvements continued after that.

It required hundreds of workers, and it cost a fortune. The modern equivalent would be a moon shot.

That huge building was erected by people who lived in wooden huts with straw roofs, people who slept on the floor because only the rich had beds.

The towers are 226 feet high, yet the builders did not have the mathematics to calculate the stresses in such structures. They proceeded by trial and error, and they made mistakes. Sometimes their work collapsed: Beauvais Cathedral fell down twice.

We take for granted our ability to go to a hardware store and buy a perfectly balanced hammer with a steel head for a few pounds, but the tools of the cathedral builders were crude, and steel was so expensive that it was used very sparingly, often for only the tip of a blade.

Notre-Dame and all cathedrals were richly decorated, yet the builders wore simple homespun tunics. The cathedral owned gold and silver plates and chalices, crucifixes and candlesticks, while the congregation drank from wooden cups and burned smoky rush lights.

How did this happen? How did such majestic beauty arise out of the violence and filth of the Middle Ages?

The first part of the answer is something almost always left out of any history of cathedrals: the weather.

The years 950 to 1250 CE are known among

climatologists as the Medieval Climatic Anomaly. For three hundred years the weather in the North Atlantic region was better than usual. The evidence comes from tree rings, ice cores and lake deposits, all of which tell us about long-term weather changes in the past. There were still occasional years of bad harvests and famine, but on average the temperature was higher. Warm weather meant more crops and wealthier people. And so Europe emerged from the long depression known as the Dark Ages.

Whenever human beings manage to produce more than they need to survive, someone comes along to take the surplus away from them. In medieval Europe there were two such groups: the aristocracy and the Church. The noblemen fought wars and, between battles, went hunting to maintain their equestrian skills and their bloodthirsty spirit. The Church built cathedrals. Bishop Maurice had money for his project – or, at least, to begin it.

He hired a master-builder, someone whose name we don't know, and the master produced a design. But this was not drawn on paper. The art of making paper was new to Europe in the twelfth century and the product was an expensive luxury. Books such as the Bible were written on parchment, which is a fine leather, also expensive.

Masons drew their designs on a tracing floor. Mortar was spread on the ground and allowed to harden, then the plans were drawn with a sharply pointed iron instrument like a nail. At first the scratch lines were white, but they faded over time, allowing new designs to be drawn on top of the old. Some tracing floors have survived, and I have studied them at York Minster and Wells Cathedral.

There would have been long discussions between Bishop Maurice and his master-mason, as the bishop explained what he wanted – a modern church filled with light – and the mason figured out how the dream could be achieved. Even so, both knew that as building progressed the design would be modified over the years by new ideas and new people.

The height of the projected building may have been an important subject of these meetings. According to the historian Jean Gimpel, in *The Cathedral Builders*, every town wanted to have the highest church:

The young medieval society represented by the bourgeoisie,
in its enthusiasm, was seized by the 'world record' fad,
and sent the naves soaring towards the sky.

The nave of Notre-Dame would be 108 feet high – the tallest in the world (though not for long: it was overtaken by Chartres a few years later).

Meanwhile the old cathedral was coming down. Its materials were not discarded, though. The best of the stones were stacked on the site to form the foundations of the new church. Even the debris was kept, because the wall of a medieval cathedral is a sandwich of two skins of dressed stone with a filling of rubble.

More stone was ordered. This was not the famous creamy-grey 'Paris stone', technically Lutetian limestone, used for the Louvre, the Invalides, the Hollywood homes of movie millionaires, and for Giorgio Armani's stores all over the world today. That was not discovered until the seventeenth century, and comes from quarries twenty-five miles north of Paris in the Department of the Oise. In the Middle Ages the cost of transporting stone could be prohibitive.

Notre-Dame used limestone from numerous quarries close to hand, just outside the boundaries of Paris.

The master would have separated stones of different characteristics: harder ones were used for structural supports that needed to bear enormous weights; softer, more easily carved stones were kept for non-load-bearing decorative details.

Once the design was finalized, the builders needed an agreed system of measurement. A yard, a pound and a gallon were not the same everywhere. Each building site had its own yardstick, an iron rod that told every worker exactly how long a yard should be.

By this time the city of Paris must have had its own standard measures, on display near the quayside on the right bank of the Seine. Paris was already a commercial city, probably the largest in Europe, and it was important to such places that a yard of cloth, a pound of silver or a gallon of wine should be the same size in every shop in town, so that customers knew what they were buying. (No doubt there were also merchants who complained about too much government regulation!) So it's likely that the master-mason of Notre-Dame made his yardstick the same as that of the merchants of Paris.

With a design on the tracing floor and a yardstick in his hand, the master-mason laid out the shape of the cathedral on the ground where the old church had stood, and building could begin.

Suddenly Paris needed more craftsmen and labourers, especially masons, carpenters and mortar-makers. There were some resident in the city, but not enough for this ambitious new project. However, cathedral builders were nomads, travelling from city to city throughout Europe in search of work (and, as they did so, spreading technical innovations and new styles). As the word got around that Paris was building a cathedral, they began to come in from the provinces and beyond, from Italy and the Netherlands and England.

There were women as well as men. Jean Gimpel, mentioned earlier, read the thirteenth-century tax register of the municipality of Paris and found many female names on the list of craftspeople who paid taxes. Gimpel was the first historian to note the role of women in building our great cathedrals. The idea that women are too weak for this kind of work is nonsense, but it might be true that the structure of the male arm is better designed for the hammering action. In any event, women were plasterers and mortar-makers more often than hammer-and-chisel masons. They frequently worked as part of a family team, husband and wife and older children, and it is easy to imagine the man cutting stone, the woman making mortar, and the teenagers fetching and carrying sand, lime and water.

Most cathedrals were built by an international effort. The designer of England's premier cathedral, Canterbury, was a Frenchman, Guillaume de Sens. Men and women of different nations worked side by side on these building sites, and foreigners are right to see Notre-Dame as their heritage as well as that of the French nation.

The work was dangerous. Once the wall grew taller than the mason, he had to work on a platform, and as the wall rose higher, so did the platform. Medieval scaffolding was a precarious construction of branches tied together with rope, and medieval people drank a great deal of ale. Guillaume de Sens fell off the scaffolding at Canterbury and died, and he was one of many.

The builders of Notre-Dame started at the east end, as usual. There was a practical reason for this. As soon as the choir was finished, the priests could start holding services there, while the rest of the church was going up.

But the construction of Notre-Dame went badly. We don't know why, though money was the commonest cause of building delays. (Other causes might include strikes, disruption of supplies and collapses.) When funds ran low, artisans would be laid off, and the work would proceed slowly until more money came in. It was nineteen years before the high altar was consecrated.

Even then the choir was not finished, because cracks appeared in the stones. The master-mason decided that the vault was too heavy. However, the solution was a happy one: to reinforce the walls, he added the elegant flying buttresses that today make the view from the east so enchanting, like a flock of birds rising into the air.

From then on the work went even more slowly.

While Chartres Cathedral was rising fast only fifty miles away, Notre-Dame went on in fits and starts.

New styles emerged. The rose windows, perhaps the best-loved features of Notre-Dame, were a late addition, begun in the 1240s by the first mason whose name we know, Jean de Chelles. The stained glass was made late in the building process, when the structure was firmly established.

The twin towers were in place by 1250. Probably the last phase was the casting of the bells. As these were well-nigh impossible to transport over any distance, they were cast on site, and the builders of Notre-Dame probably made a bell pit near the base of the west front, so that the finished article could be hauled up directly into the tower.

The cathedral was more or less built by 1260. But Bishop Maurice had died in 1196. He never saw his great cathedral finished.

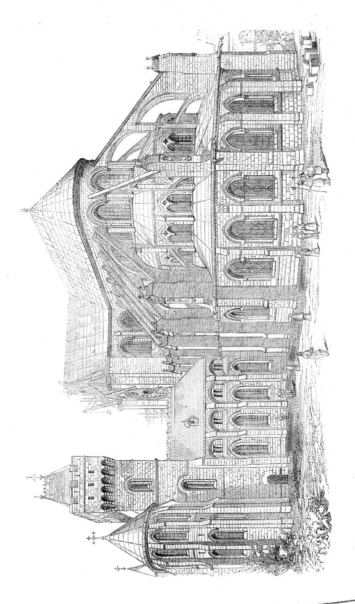

Notre-Dame after completion

3

1831

At the age of twenty-nine, Victor Hugo was a famous poet. As a young man he had written two novels but they had not been very successful, and few people read them today. However, his plays had caused a stir. *Marion de Lorme* was suppressed by the censor and *Hernani* was so scandalous that it provoked rioting in the theatre of the Comédie-Française.

Hugo represented one side in a literary controversy: the conflict between Classicists and Romantics. It's a dispute which seems, to modern readers, as pointless as the medieval argument about how many angels can dance on the head of a pin; but in nineteenth-century Paris it got intellectuals sufficiently riled up to punch one another. Hugo was seen as a representative of the Romantics.

Paradoxically, the young poet was a conservative in politics. Born in the aftermath of the French Revolution, he wanted to see the French monarchy restored. The revolutionaries had rejected all religion – they had turned Notre-Dame into a 'Temple of Reason', and they had venerated the Goddess of Reason, often depicted as a woman revealingly draped in the red, white and blue colours of the French flag. But young Hugo believed in the authority of the

Liberty Leading the People,
by Eugène Delacroix

Catholic Church. He even founded a magazine called *The Literary Conservative*.

However, he changed. He wrote in his diary: 'In the last ten years my former royalist and Catholic conviction of 1820 has crumbled piece by piece before age and experience.' He produced a short semi-fictional work called *The Last Day of a Condemned Man*, a strikingly compassionate account of the final hours of a man condemned to death, based on a real-life murderer. He was beginning to see French society as sometimes harsh and cruel, and his imagination was more and more occupied by the despised: prisoners, orphans, cripples, beggars and murderers. And like every novelist he burned to transform his obsessions into stories. He was moving rapidly towards the social criticism that thirty years later would produce his masterpiece, *Les Misérables*.

He had long ago taken an advance from a publisher for a historical novel set in Paris, and he had done a lot of research; but he kept postponing the actual writing. His publisher was at first forgiving, as they usually are, but eventually became more insistent, as they usually do.

On 1 September 1830 he sat down to write Chapter One. His wife recalled: 'He bought himself a bottle of ink and a huge grey knitted shawl, which covered him from head to foot; locked away his formal clothes, so that he would not be tempted to go out; and entered his novel as if it were a prison.' (Writers are often swathed in wool, by the way; we sit still all day, so we get cold.)

By the middle of January 1831 the book was, astonishingly, finished. He had written something like 180,000 words in four and a half months. And it was very, very good.

Set in the year 1482, it had the same name as the cathedral, *Notre-Dame de Paris*. The heroine is Esmeralda, a beautiful gypsy girl who dances in the street for pennies. The three other major characters are men who fall in love with her: the penniless student Pierre Gringoire, the haughty archdeacon Claude Frollo and the deformed bell-ringer Quasimodo.

It got poor reviews but the public loved it, and it was quickly translated into other languages. The English edition was called *The Hunchback of Notre-*

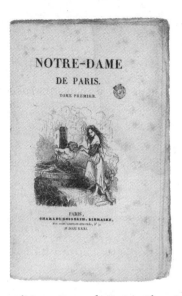

Title page of Notre-Dame de Paris *with a vignette by*
Tony Johannot, Paris, edited by Gosselin, 1831

Dame, a title at once more vulgar and more alluring.
And Hugo became world-famous.

Hugo admired the work of Walter Scott, often said
to be the inventor of the historical novel; but he wrote,
in a review of *Quentin Durward*, that the genre could
do more. He did not say that he could write better
than Scott, but he surely thought it, and to my mind
he was right. Hugo would never produce a sentence

as constipated as this, picked almost at random from Scott's *Waverley*:

> The drawing-room of Flora Mac-Ivor was furnished in the plainest and most simple manner; for at Glennaquoich every other sort of expenditure was retrenched as much as possible, for the purpose of maintaining, in its full dignity, the hospitality of the chieftain, and retaining and multiplying the number of his dependants and adherents.

Hugo wanted to write more like Homer, author of the central works of Greek literature, the *Odyssey* and the *Iliad*. He created works of colour and grandeur and passion that, to my mind, make Walter Scott pale by comparison.

Notre-Dame de Paris takes the reader into the criminal underworld, whose filth and violence Hugo describes with a mixture of disgust and relish that cannot help but remind us of his contemporary Charles Dickens. This fascination with low life was hugely successful among readers, and it spawned imitators. Eugène Sue's vividly sensational *The Mysteries of Paris* was more popular than Hugo's novel in the short term. Sue's work was published in 150 instalments on the front page of the newspaper *Journal des Débats*. It captured the imagination of the nation, being read aloud in factories and offices, cafes and bars. However, it lacked the timeless distinction of Hugo's work, and is hardly ever read today.

Many of Hugo's characters are preposterously larger than life, teetering dangerously on the cliff-edge of absurdity. As well as those already mentioned, we meet the vicious king of the thieves Clopin Trouillefou; the hermit Sister Gudule, who lives walled up in self-imprisonment for years; the judge Florian Barbedienne, who issues random verdicts because he is stone deaf and has no idea what is going on in his court; and the hopelessly dissolute Jehan Frollo.

In the twenty-first century we believe that people who are different from the average should not be defined by their difference, but seen in the round. Novelists have never worked that way: rather, they use differences to express personality. Shylock and Fagin are defined by their Jewishness; Captain Hook and Blind Pugh are defined by their disability; and the list of characters defined by their sexual orientation is very long – E. M. Forster's Maurice, Patricia Highsmith's Carol, George R. R. Martin's Renly Baratheon, Ian Fleming's Pussy Galore, and many more.

Quasimodo is defined by his ugliness:

In fact he was wicked because he was feral, and he was feral because he was ugly.

In order to tell his highly coloured tale of angry confrontations and incessant crises, Hugo developed a style of extraordinary vividness and power, muscular enough to carry the weight of all that melodrama. The greatest and most popular novelists, from Jane Austen to Ian Fleming, have often created highly individual prose tailored to suit the material of their stories.

The quality of Hugo's writing is well illustrated by a passage in which he imagines, with spooky prescience, a fire at Notre-Dame:

All eyes were lifted to the heights of the church. What they saw was extraordinary. At the top of the highest gallery, above the rose window, a tall flame rose between the two bell towers with a tornado of sparks, a tall flame reckless and angry, from time to time shredded into the smoke by the wind. Below this flame, below the dark balustrade with its glowing leaves, two gutters vomited relentlessly through monster mouths a hard rain that gleamed silver against the dark façade. As they approached the ground, the two jets of liquid lead widened into multiple streamlets, like the spray from the thousand holes of a watering-can. Above the flame, the vast towers, each harsh and sharply carved, one all black, the other all red, seemed even bigger because of the immense shadow they cast up to the sky. The innumerable sculptures of devils and dragons took on a dismal look. The restless brightness of the flames made them seem to fidget. There were laughing vipers, yapping gargoyles, salamanders fanning the fire with their breath, and monsters that sneezed in the smoke.

No one had ever written like this before.

The novel that Notre-Dame inspired Hugo to write has been made into at least thirteen films, five television series, five plays, fifteen stage musicals, five ballets, two BBC radio serials and a video game, according to Wikipedia. There may be many more versions. Probably the most distinguished film is the 1939 black-and-white version starring Charles Laughton as Quasimodo. I remember seeing it as a boy, on someone's tiny 1960s television set, and being scared stiff.

Hugo's novel swept the world; but it did more.

Nineteenth-century novelists felt free to stop the story and insert a long passage of barely relevant description and opinion. There are many in *Notre-Dame de Paris*, but the most passionate are about the cathedral.

At the beginning of Book Three Hugo wrote:

> *The church of Notre-Dame de Paris is still today a majestic and sublime building. But, beautifully though it has aged, we must sigh, and we must feel outraged at the degradation and mutilation that time and men have inflicted on this awesome monument . . .*

Hugo was angry about this. Notre-Dame had been much abused during the French Revolution and afterwards. Its statuary had been damaged and its nave had been used as a grain store.

Both Hugo's eulogistic descriptions of the beauty of Notre-Dame and his outraged protests about its dereliction moved the readers of his book. A worldwide bestseller, it attracted tourists and pilgrims to the cathedral, and the half-ruined building they saw shamed the city of Paris. His indignation spread to others. The government decided to do something.

A competition was held to choose the expert who would supervise the renovation of the cathedral. Two young architects collaborated on the winning proposal. One of them died suddenly, but the other went on to do the work. His name was Eugène Viollet-le-Duc.

He was thirty when he won the job, and he would be fifty before it was finished.

4

1844

Eugène Viollet-le-Duc

Viollet-le-Duc came from a family steeped in French high culture: his grandfather was an architect; his uncle was a painter who studied under the great David;

and his father was governor of the royal residences.

All his adult life Viollet-le-Duc visited medieval buildings, drew them beautifully and theorized about architecture. His writings and drawings are collected in the *Encyclopédie Médiévale*, a massive volume full of detail and insight. With his mentor Prosper Mérimée, he worked on the restoration of numerous buildings including Sainte-Chapelle, a royal church that had been built around the same time as Notre-Dame on the Île de la Cité.

He loved his job. Looking back, he said: 'Work was the best part of our day.' He was obsessed with medieval architecture, and he adored the Cathedral of Notre-Dame de Paris. There was no one in the world better qualified to renovate Notre-Dame.

He began by meticulously making a colour-coded map showing the location and type of every stone in the areas needing repair.

Labourers began to remove the damaged stones. The statues over the west portals had been beheaded during the revolution, and more than sixty had to be replaced. Other decorative features such as gargoyles and chimaeras – monstrous animals – had been smashed.

As they were taken down, Viollet-le-Duc made drawings of what was left, displaying the painstaking draughtsmanship which must have been a reflection of his innermost character. I am the proud owner of one of those drawings. It shows a corbel, which is a support for a shaft, carved as the head of an imaginary monster.

Eugène Viollet-le-Duc, 'Sketch for a corbel decoration for restoration of Notre-Dame de Paris', 1848

He also exploited the new technology of photography to make daguerreotypes:

*Viollet-le-Duc's daguerreotype photograph of
the west front of Notre-Dame*

Where there was nothing left but an empty space, he used drawings and photographs from other medieval cathedrals to design substitutes. He drew Gothic windows to replace the medieval stained glass broken in the revolution.

Viollet-le-Duc replaced those of the bells that had been melted down for cannons in the revolution. (The great Emmanuel had somehow survived.) In the north tower he put a new, stronger timber support structure; and as I watched with horrified eyes on 15 April 2019, I thought I saw fire inside that tower. Later reports said those flames had been extinguished just in time by firemen who had bravely ascended the tower at the risk of their lives.

Viollet-le-Duc put together a team of skilled masons, carpenters, sculptors and glaziers to repair or reproduce the impaired stonework.

His aim was to restore the church to its original look, but he was not sufficiently meticulous to satisfy the most conservative critics. His gargoyles were not very medieval, they complained, and the chimaeras that he created to decorate the roof were not like anything else in the church. The ambulatory and the chapels that radiate from it were said to be over-decorated, an unusual fault to find with a Gothic cathedral, a bit like saying that a party frock is too pretty. The restored south rose window has some of the figures in the wrong order, apparently.

Worst of all, the new spire was positively modern.

The medieval cathedral had had a central tower with a spire. Victor Hugo described it as 'this charming little bell tower', although he never saw it: it was dismantled before he was born. He wrote angrily of the architect who removed it, but in all likelihood it had become weak and was in danger of being blown down.

As far as I know, there is no reliable description of the original tower, just two sketches. In any event Viollet-le-Duc made no attempt to imitate a medieval tower in his design for the replacement, and this is the loudest complaint of his critics. Instead, he modelled the new spire on a similar one recently added to the cathedral at Orléans. At its base were images of three disciples, and it was said that the face of Saint Thomas staring up at the spire looked remarkably like that of Viollet-le-Duc himself.

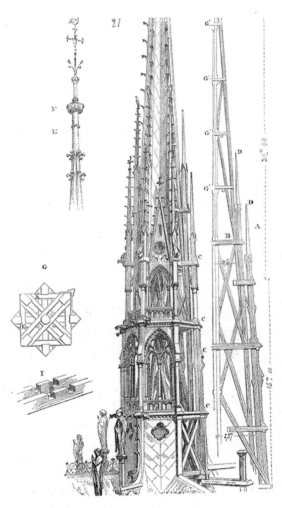

Viollet-le-Duc's drawing of the spire for Notre-Dame

Notre-Dame's spire under construction, around 1860

The criticism did him no harm. He spent the rest of his life as the leading expert in his field. He was consulted on the repair and renovation of dozens of buildings, and he wrote copiously on theories of architecture. He seemed to have no end of energy. In his sixties he was elected to the Paris city council. He died at the age of sixty-five after spending the summer hiking in the Alps.

*The consecration of Notre-Dame following
the restoration by Eugène Viollet-le-Duc, 1864*

5

1944

The chapel of Saint Joseph is half-way along the south side of the nave. In 1944 it contained a statue of Joseph holding the baby Jesus. On 26 August, the morning after Paris was liberated, Mass was said in the chapel in English by a bespectacled American priest, Father Leonard Fries, wearing borrowed French robes.

The chapel is less than 130 square feet, and contained an altar as well as the statue, but the service was attended by three hundred men, mostly of the US Army 12th Infantry Regiment, all carrying carbines or full-length rifles and holding their helmets in their hands. They overflowed into the aisle and the nave of the great cathedral. As the sun rose into a cloudless sky and shone through the stained glass of the east end, some of the men who had freed Paris knelt to remember the comrades they had left behind on the beaches of Normandy.

It was the first service that day, but later there would be another, much bigger. The radio that morning announced that General Charles de Gaulle would lead a victory march along the Champs-Élysées at 2 p.m. and attend a thanksgiving service of Te Deum at 4.30 p.m. in the Cathedral of Notre-Dame.

De Gaulle had been head of the provisional French government in exile and was determined to become the new leader of the liberated country, but his right to do so was debatable. He was at odds with the Resistance leaders, who had stayed to fight the Germans in France while he was living at the Connaught Hotel in London. Now he was determined to position himself as *de facto* president. When Napoleon crowned himself Emperor of the French on 2 December 1804, he did it at Notre-Dame. And de Gaulle knew that if he was going to make himself look like France's new ruler, he needed to do it in Notre-Dame.

His unilateral announcement of a victory parade infuriated the Allies. Paris was not yet secure.

There were still German soldiers in the city. US general Leonard Gerow had ordered the French 2nd Armoured Division to guard the north-east suburbs against a possible German counter-attack, but he was told that de Gaulle, ignoring the chain of command, had commandeered the division for his parade.

De Gaulle outmanoeuvred the Resistance and the Allied command, and he got his parade.

De Gaulle had also failed to ask anyone's permission to hold a service in the cathedral, but Cardinal Emmanuel Suhard, the archbishop of Paris, was merely the next authority to crumble before the irresistible force of de Gaulle's will.

At about the same time, General Alfred Jodl in Germany placed a call to Army Group B at Margival in France and asked for Field Marshal Walter Model. The field marshal was not in the underground bunker, so Jodl spoke to General Hans Speidel. Repeating Hitler's personal instructions, Jodl ordered a massive V-bomb attack on Paris that night.

Speidel never passed the message on. A week later he was arrested by the Gestapo.

De Gaulle was late for the parade, but no one cared.

He arrived at ten past three at the Arc de Triomphe. Acting as if he were already the head of state, he lit the eternal flame and laid a wreath of red gladioli on the Tomb of the Unknown Soldier. Then he turned and looked along the Champs-Élysées.

Thousands of Parisians, dozens of journalists and several film cameras were waiting for him. The spectators crowded the sidewalks of the broad boulevard, climbed the chestnut trees, leaned from windows and balconies, and even stood on the rooftops, waving flags and banners, all the way to the Obelisk.

A group of several hundred men and women broke through the crowd onto the road dressed in seventeenth-century costume, the women draped in red, white and blue, and topless like the goddess in Delacroix's painting. Having made their point, whatever it was, they vanished again.

Before ordering the parade to move off, de Gaulle gave one more vital instruction: he told his entourage that they should all take care to remain at least one step behind him for the entire march.

Then, unmistakably the hero of the hour, he set off at the head of the procession.

Charles de Gaulle walking down the Champs-Élysées
on his way to Notre-Dame

De Gaulle reached the Place de la Concorde and was approaching an open-top Hotchkiss – a French-made luxury car – that stood waiting to take him onward to Notre-Dame when shots were heard.

Thousands of spectators threw themselves flat or took cover behind the vehicles of the 2nd Armoured Division. Stretcher-bearers dressed in white ran into the crowd to see to the casualties.

No one knew who was firing. It was probably

German snipers left behind in the city, but it might have been Resistance fighters angry that they were not leading the parade, or Communists opposed to de Gaulle's takeover.

De Gaulle was impervious. He did not duck or take cover or even pause in his stately progress. He might easily have been killed, and clearly he was prepared to risk death at this crucial moment in his career and in the history of France. He climbed into the open car, ordered the driver on, and sat waving to the crowds, unprotected, all the way to the Île de la Cité.

It was a masterpiece of political theatre. Fearless, dignified and strong-willed – and six foot five inches tall – he appeared exactly the man to drive France's post-war recovery. Films and photographs of his performance were all over the world within hours.

As he arrived in front of the Cathedral of Notre-Dame, more shots rang out. Snipers had got into the north tower.

In reply, the French soldiers of the 2nd Armoured Division raked the tower and the rooftop with fire, sending fragments of limestone flying off the statues so carefully restored by Viollet-le-Duc. De Gaulle, unheeding, stepped out of his car and received a bouquet – red, white and blue flowers – from a scared but brave little girl. Then he entered by the Portal of the Last Judgement.

Most of the congregation were on the floor as gunfire rang out in the nave. 'One could see more bottoms than faces,' an observer said later. De Gaulle did not change his pace. His seat was one hundred and ninety feet away down the nave, and he walked the entire distance with a majestically slow step.

As he reached his place, General Marie-Pierre Koenig, commander of the French Forces of the Interior, bellowed at the congregation: 'Stand up!'

The priest sang the opening words of the Magnificat: 'My soul magnifies the Lord.'

And then the nave echoed with the sound of the people of Paris singing.

6

1989

Every year, millions of people visit Notre-Dame and other cathedrals. They are the oldest buildings in north-west Europe. There are even more ancient buildings elsewhere – Roman ruins, Greek temples, the Egyptian pyramids – but I think our cathedrals are the oldest still used for their original purpose.

The cathedrals have always attracted tourists. Today's visitors come not just from Europe but from very different cultures, including Japan, the United States and India. When all these visitors look at our cathedrals, what do they think?

We often catch our first glimpse from a distance. As at Chartres, the towers of the church appear over the horizon when we are still miles away. The medieval visitor must have been awestruck by the sight, as he was meant to be.

Our next reaction, as we come closer, is often confusion. It seems too complicated to understand. It's a bit like the first time you hear a Beethoven symphony. There are so many melodies, rhythms, instruments and harmonies that at first you can't grasp how they are linked and interrelated. It is hard to see the logic. A cathedral, like a symphony, has a coherent plan, its windows and arches form rhythms, its decorations have themes and tell stories, but the whole thing is so rich that at first it overwhelms us.

When we step inside, this changes. Most people experience a sense of tranquillity. The cool air, the ancient stones, the regular repetitions of the architecture and the way the entire building seems to reach toward heaven all work together to soothe the human soul.

The first thing most of us do inside the cathedral is buy a guide book. This may tell us that the site was a place of worship before Christianity was invented. Notre-Dame was the location of a temple to the Roman god Jupiter.

Often we learn that the church was not built all at once, the way a modern skyscraper or shopping mall would be. We may find that the early Christians had a wooden church, of which nothing now remains. Notre-Dame is the fifth church built on the site. Often the building of the current church began when the old one burned down. Sometimes the chapter ran out of money, and work halted for a hundred years.

At the end of a visit to a cathedral, if we're lucky, we no longer feel confused. We know something of the gradual process by which the church was built. We see the arches and windows as solutions to technical problems as well as objects of beauty. Perhaps we have begun to learn the iconography, the process of interpretation by which anonymous statues of apparently similar angels and saints turn into Bible stories. Understanding the groups of statuary over a doorway is very like deciphering a picture by Picasso. We say, 'Ah, of course, that must be Saint Stephen,' just as after studying a Picasso for a while we may say: 'Of course, there is her elbow, sticking out of her head.'

But we are left with more questions.

Readers sometimes ask: How do you know so much about the medieval builders? Some of our information comes from pictures. When medieval artists made illustrations for Bibles they often depicted the Tower of Babel. The story, in the Book of Genesis, is that men decided to build a tower up to heaven, and their arrogance displeased God, who made them all speak different languages, so that in the resulting confusion the project was abandoned. Those illustrations, showing stonemasons and mortar-makers, scaffolding and hoists, give us a lot of evidence about medieval building sites.

Other sources of information about cathedral builders include surviving contracts between the chapter and the builders, for example, and payroll records. One of the books that inspired me to write *The Pillars of the Earth* is *The Cathedral Builders* (*Les bâtisseurs de cathédrales*) by Jean Gimpel, whom I mentioned earlier. When I began work on *Pillars*, I decided to get in touch with Gimpel and ask him to be a historical consultant for my novel. I knew that the Gimpels were a famous French family of art dealers and I assumed he would live in Paris. However, not only did he live in London but in my street. He agreed to be one of my consultants for *Pillars*, and all he asked for in payment was a case of champagne. We became friends and table-tennis opponents, and he beat me every week.

When I began *Pillars* in January 1986, I wanted to understand, for myself, and to explain, for readers, how and why the medieval cathedrals were built, and why they look the way they do. I hope *Pillars* shows how the construction of a cathedral served the different interests of each major power group in medieval society: monarchy, aristocracy, priesthood, traders, townspeople and peasants.

In March of 1989 I wrote 'The End' on the last page of *The Pillars of the Earth*. It had taken me three years and three months to write, and I had been thinking about it much longer.

I was not the first author to be inspired by cathedrals. Victor Hugo was the greatest, to my mind. Anthony Trollope made the fictional Barchester Cathedral the centre of a six-novel series, the Chronicles of Barsetshire. William Golding won the Nobel Prize for an oeuvre that included *The Spire*, a dizzying story of a priest's obsession with building a four-hundred-foot spire on top of a cathedral that has no proper foundations. T. S. Eliot wrote a verse play, *Murder in the Cathedral*, about the assassination in 1170 of Thomas Becket, the archbishop of Canterbury. Raymond Carver wrote a story called *Cathedral* about a blind man drawing a cathedral, and Nelson de Mille wrote a thriller, also called *Cathedral*, about the IRA taking over St Patrick's Cathedral on Fifth Avenue in New York.

Each of us was enraptured by something different. I saw the building of the cathedral as the kind of communal enterprise that captures the imagination of an entire society. A cathedral is a work of art, but it was never the brainchild of one person. Although there was always a master-mason who drew the basic designs, he relied for the detailed work on a small army of artists and craftsmen, all of whom had their own talents and used their own imaginations. In some ways he was like the producer of a movie, who manages actors, writers, set designers, costume makers, make-up artists and lighting specialists, and tries to get each of them to give the best of what his or her genius has to offer. For me, the cathedral is about what people can achieve when they work together.

Furthermore, this work of art could not be made unless thousands more people supported the project. It was the achievement of an entire community. In *Pillars* I wrote about how the building of the cathedral drew in people from every sector of medieval society: not just the clergy but aristocrats, business people, city dwellers and rural agriculturalists. They gave support and money, a lot of money. Everyone benefited. Employment was created, commerce was strengthened, markets grew up, international migration was stimulated, and new technology was constantly being invented and spread. In my novel, those who oppose the building do so only because they want it built somewhere else.

I have compared the building of a cathedral to a space launch. It involved the whole of society in the same way, it developed cutting-edge technology, it brought widespread economic benefits – and yet when you add up all the pragmatic reasons, they're not quite enough to explain why we did it. There is another element, which is the spiritual, a human being's need to aspire to something above the material life. When you've seen how each group in Kingsbridge serves its own interests, you haven't yet grasped the full picture. *Pillars* explains that it was also done for the glory of God.

Not long ago I was on the roof of Peterborough Cathedral. Some of the pinnacles had been replaced in the 1950s, and I noticed that the new ones were crude, lacking detail, by comparison with the highly decorated medieval features beside them. The difference was not visible from the ground, and evidently the craftsmen of the 1950s thought there was no point in carving details that no one could see. The medieval builders would have disagreed. They made the unseen parts just as carefully as those on public view because, after all, God could see them.

A journalist asked me: 'Don't you hate all the tourists in their shorts with their cameras?' No. Cathedrals have always been full of tourists. In the Middle Ages they were not called tourists, they were pilgrims, but they travelled for many of the same reasons: to see the world and its marvels, to broaden their minds, to educate themselves, and perhaps to come into touch with something miraculous, otherworldly, eternal.

I believe that a novel is successful to the extent that it touches the emotions of the reader. And something similar may be true of all works of art. It is certainly true of cathedrals. Our encounters with them are emotional. When we see them, we are awestruck. When we walk around, we are enraptured by their grace and light. When we sit quietly, we are possessed by a sense of peace.

And when one burns, we weep.

Written 19–26 April 2019 in
Knebworth, England

Acknowledgements

The first draft of this essay was read and helpfully criticized by John Clare, Barbara Follett and *l'équipe française* – Cécile Boyer-Runge, Claire Do Sêrro, Maggie Doyle and Marine Alata at Éditions Robert Laffont. I am grateful to them all.

Picture Acknowledgements

Page 9 © Program33/France.TV/*The Secrets of the Builders: Notre-Dame* by Emmanuel Blanchard

Page 11 Bishop Saint, c. 1425 by Fra Angelico, church of San Domenico, Fiesole, Italy © Metropolitan Museum of Art, New York, USA/Bridgeman Images

Page 23 © AKG Images/De Agostini/Biblioteca Ambrosiana

Page 26 Liberty Leading the People, 28 July 1830, c. 1830–31 by Eugène Delacroix © Louvre-Lens, France/Bridgeman Images

Page 29 © Carole Rabourdin/Library of Victor Hugo's house/Roger-Viollet

Page 37 © Franck/Tallandier/Bridgeman Images

Page 39 Author's private collection

Page 40 © Museum of the History of Science, Broad Street, Oxford, England

Page 43 Author's private collection

Page 44 © Musée Carnavalet/Roger-Viollet

Page 45 © Granger/Bridgeman Images

Page 51 © The Imperial War Museums collection

INTERNATIONAL NO. 1 BESTSELLER
KEN FOLLETT RETURNS WITH

The Evening and the Morning

A thrilling and addictive novel from the master of
historical fiction, publishing in September 2020.

A journey that will end where
The Pillars of the Earth begins . . .

An exclusive extract follows here.

I

Thursday, 17 June 997

It was hard to stay awake all night, Edgar found, even on the most important night of your life.

He had spread his cloak over the reeds on the floor and now he lay on it, dressed in the knee-length brown wool tunic that was all he wore in summer, day and night. In winter he would wrap the cloak around him and lie near the fire. But now the weather was warm: Midsummer's Day was a week away.

Edgar always knew dates. Most people had to ask priests, who kept calendars. Edgar's elder brother Erman had once said to him: 'How come you know when Easter is?' and he had replied: 'Because it's the first Sunday after the first full moon after the twenty-first day of March, obviously.' It had been a mistake to add 'obviously', because Erman had punched him in the stomach for being sarcastic. That had been years ago, when Edgar was small. He was grown now: he would be eighteen three days after Midsummer. His brothers no longer punched him.

He shook his head. Random thoughts sent him drifting off. He tried to make himself uncomfortable, lying on his fist to stay awake. He should have brought a stone to put under his head as a comfortless pillow, but then someone might have asked what he was up to.

He wondered how much longer he had to wait.

He turned his head and looked around by firelight. His home was like almost every other house in the town of Combe: oak plank walls, a thatched roof and an earth floor partly covered with reeds from the banks of the nearby river. It had no windows. In the middle of the single room was a square of stones surrounding the hearth. Over the fire stood an iron tripod from which cooking pots could be hung, and its legs made spidery shadows on the underside of the roof. All around the walls were wooden pegs on which were hung clothes, cooking utensils and boatbuilding tools.

Edgar was not sure how much of the night had passed, because he might have dozed off, perhaps more than once. Earlier, he had listened to the sounds of the town settling for the night: a couple of drunks singing an obscene ditty, the bitter accusations of a marital quarrel in a neighbouring house, a door slamming and a dog barking and, somewhere nearby, a woman sobbing. But now there was nothing but the soft lullaby of waves on a sheltered beach. He stared in the direction of the door, looking for telltale lines of light around its edges, and saw only darkness. That meant either that the moon had set, so the night was well advanced, or that the sky was cloudy, which would tell him nothing.

The rest of his family lay around the room, close to the walls where there was less smoke. Pa and Ma were back to back. Sometimes they would wake in the middle of the night and embrace, whispering and moving together, until they fell back, panting; but they were fast asleep now, Pa snoring. Erman, the eldest brother at twenty, lay near Edgar, and Eadbald, the middle one, was in the corner. Edgar could hear their steady, untroubled breathing.

At last, the church bell struck.

There was a monastery on the far side of the town. The monks had a way of measuring the hours of the night: they made big graduated candles that told the time as they burned down. One hour before dawn they would ring the bell, then get up to chant their service of matins.

Edgar lay still a little longer. The bell might have disturbed Ma, who woke easily. He gave her time to sink back into deep slumber. Then, at last, he got to his feet.

Silently he picked up his cloak, his shoes and his belt with the sheathed dagger attached. On bare feet he crossed the room, avoiding the furniture: a table, two stools and a bench. The door opened silently: Edgar had greased the wooden hinges yesterday with a generous smear of sheep's tallow.

If one of his family woke now and spoke to him, he would say he was going outside to piss, and hope they did not spot that he was carrying his shoes.

Eadbald grunted. Edgar froze. Had Eadbald woken up, or just made a noise in his sleep? Edgar could not tell. But Eadbald was the passive one, always keen to avoid a fuss, like Pa. He would not make trouble.

Edgar stepped out and closed the door behind him carefully.

The moon had set, but the sky was clear and the beach was starlit. Between the house and the high-tide mark was a boatyard. Pa was a boatbuilder, and his three sons worked with him. Pa was a good craftsman but a poor businessman, so Ma made all the money decisions, especially the difficult calculation of what price to ask for something as complicated as a boat or ship. If a customer tried to bargain down the price, Pa would be willing to give in, but Ma would make him stand firm.

Edgar glanced at the yard as he laced his shoes and buckled his belt. There was only one vessel under construction, a small boat for rowing upriver. Beside it stood a large and valuable stockpile of timber, the trunks split into halves and quarters, ready to be shaped into the parts of a boat. About once a month the whole family went into the forest and felled a mature oak tree. Pa and Edgar would begin, alternately swinging long-handled axes, cutting a precise wedge out of the trunk. Then they would rest while Erman and Eadbald took over. When the tree came down they would trim it, then float the wood downriver to Combe. They had to pay, of course: the forest belonged to Wigelm, the thane to whom most people in Combe paid their rent, and he demanded twelve silver pennies for each tree.

As well as the timber pile, the yard contained a barrel of tar, a coil of rope and a whetstone. All were guarded by a chained-up mastiff called Grendel, black with a grey muzzle, too old to do much harm to thieves but still able to bark an alarm. Grendel was quiet now, watching Edgar incuriously with his head resting on his front paws.

Edgar knelt down and stroked his head. 'Goodbye, old dog,' he murmured, and Grendel wagged his tail without getting up.

Also in the yard was one finished vessel, and Edgar thought of it as his own. He had built it himself to an original design, based on a Viking ship. Edgar had never actually seen a Viking – they had not raided Combe in his lifetime – but two years ago a wreck had washed up on the beach here, empty and fire-blackened, its dragon figurehead half smashed, presumably after some battle. Edgar had been awestruck by its mutilated beauty: the graceful curves, the long serpentine prow and the slender hull. He had been most impressed by the large out-jutting keel that ran the length of the ship, which – he had realized after some thought – gave the stability that allowed the Vikings to cross the seas. Edgar's boat was a lesser version, with two oars and a small, square sail.

Edgar knew he had a talent. He was already a better boatbuilder than his elder brothers, and before long he would overtake Pa. He had an intuitive sense of how forms fitted together to make a stable structure. Years ago he had overheard Pa say to Ma: 'Erman learns slowly and Eadbald learns fast, but Edgar seems to understand before the words are out of my mouth.' It was true. Some men could pick up a musical instrument they had never played, a pipe or a lyre, and get a tune out of it after a few minutes. Edgar had such instincts about boats, and houses too. He would say: 'That boat will list to starboard,' or, 'That roof will leak,' and he was always right.

Now he untied his boat and pushed it down the beach. The sound of the hull scraping on the sand was muffled by the shushing of the waves breaking on the shore.

He was startled by a girlish giggle. In the starlight he saw a naked woman lying on the sand, and a man on top of her. Edgar probably knew them, but their faces were not clearly visible and he looked away quickly, not wanting to recognize them. He had surprised them in an illicit tryst, he guessed. The woman seemed young and perhaps the man was married. The clergy preached against such affairs, but people did not always follow the rules. Edgar ignored the couple and pushed his boat into the water.

He glanced back at the house, feeling a pang of regret, wondering whether he would ever see it again. It was the only home he could remember. He knew, because he had been told, that he had been born in another town, Exeter, where his father had worked for a master boatbuilder; then the family had moved, while Edgar was still a baby, and had set up home in Combe, where Pa had started his own enterprise with one order for a rowboat; but Edgar could not remember any of that. This was the only home he knew, and he was leaving it for good.

He was lucky to have found employment elsewhere. Business had slowed since the renewal of Viking attacks when Edgar was nine years old. Trading and fishing were dangerous while the marauders were near. Only the brave bought boats.

There were three ships in the harbour now, he saw by starlight: two herring fishers and a Frankish merchant ship. Dragged up on the beach were a handful of smaller craft, river and coastal vessels. He had helped to build one of the fishers. But he could remember a time when there had always been a dozen or more ships in port.

He felt a fresh breeze from the south-west, the prevailing wind here. His boat had a sail – small, because they were so costly: a full-size sail for a seagoing ship would take one woman four years to make. But it was hardly worthwhile to unfurl for the short trip across the bay. He began to row, something that hardly taxed him. Edgar was heavily muscled, like a blacksmith. His father and brothers were the same. All day, six days a week, they worked with axe, adze and auger, shaping the oak strakes that formed the hulls of boats. It was hard work and it made strong men.

His heart lifted. He had got away. And he was going to meet the woman he loved. The stars were brilliant, the beach glowed white, and, when his oars broke the surface of the water, the curling foam was like the fall of her hair on her shoulders.

Her name was Sungifu, which was usually shortened to Sunni, and she was exceptional in every way.

He could see the premises along the sea front, most of them workplaces of fishermen and traders: the forge of a tinsmith who made rustproof items for ships; the long yard in which a roper wove his lines; and the huge kiln of a tar-maker who roasted pine logs to produce the sticky liquid with which boatbuilders waterproofed their vessels. The town always looked bigger from the water: it was home to a couple of thousand people, most making their living, directly or indirectly, from the sea.

He looked across the bay to his destination. In the darkness he would not have been able to see Sunni even if she had been there, which he knew she was not, since they had arranged to meet at dawn. But he could not help staring at the place where she soon would be.

Sunni was twenty-one, older than Edgar by more than three years. She had caught his attention one day when he was sitting on the beach staring at the Viking wreck. He knew her by sight, of course – he knew everyone living in the small town – but he had not particularly noticed her before, and did not recall anything about her family. 'Were you washed up with the wreck?' she had said. 'You were sitting so still, I thought you were driftwood.' She had to be imaginative, he saw right away, to say something like that off the top of her head; and he had explained what fascinated him about the lines of the vessel, feeling that she would understand. They had talked for an hour and he had fallen in love.

Then she told him she was married, but it was already too late.

Her husband, Cyneric, was thirty. She had been fourteen when she married him. He had a small herd of milk cows, and Sunni managed the dairy. She was shrewd and made plenty of money for her husband. They had no children.

Edgar had quickly learned that Sunni hated Cyneric. Every night, after the evening milking, he went to an alehouse called the Sailors and got drunk. While he was there, Sunni could slip into the woods and meet Edgar.

However, from now on there would be no more hiding. Today they would run away together – or, to be exact, sail away. Edgar had the offer of a job and a house in a fishing village fifty miles along the coast. It was a lucky break: few boatbuilders were hiring, but this one was busy, and he had seen Edgar's work and liked it. Edgar had no money – he never had money; Ma said he had no need of it – but his tools were in a locker built into the boat. They would start a new life.

As soon as everyone realized they had gone, Cyneric would consider himself free to marry again. A wife who ran away with another man was, in practice, divorcing herself; the Church might not like it, but that was the custom. Within a few weeks, Sunni said, Cyneric would go into the countryside and find a desperately poor family with a pretty fourteen-year-old daughter. Edgar wondered why the man wanted a wife: he had little interest in sex, according to Sunni. 'He likes to have someone to push around,' she had said. 'My problem was that I grew old enough to despise him.'

Cyneric would not come after them, even if he found out where they were, which was unlikely, at least for some time to come. 'And if we're wrong about that, and Cyneric finds us, I'll beat the shit out of him,' Edgar had said. Sunni's expression had told him that she thought this was a foolish boast, and he knew she was right. Hastily, he had added: 'But it probably won't come to that.'

He reached the far side of the bay, then beached the boat and roped it to a boulder.

He could hear the chanting of the monks at their prayers. The monastery was nearby, and the home of Cyneric and Sunni a few hundred yards beyond that.

He sat on the sand, looking out at the dark sea and the night sky, thinking about her. Would she be able to slip away as easily as he had? What if Cyneric woke up and prevented her from leaving? There might be a fight; she could be beaten. He was suddenly tempted to change the plan, get up from the beach and go to her house and fetch her.

He repressed the urge with an effort. She was better off on her own. Cyneric would be in a drunken slumber and Sunni would move like a cat. She had planned to go to bed wearing around her neck her only item of jewellery, an intricately carved silver roundel hanging from a leather thong. In her belt pouch she would have a useful needle and thread and the embroidered linen headband she wore on special occasions. Like Edgar, she could be out of the house in a few silent seconds.

Soon she would be here, her eyes glistening with excitement, her supple body eager for his. They would embrace, hugging each other hard, and kiss passionately; then she would step into the boat and he would push it into the water to freedom. He would row a little way out, then kiss her again, he thought. How soon could they make love? She would be as impatient as he. He could row around the point, then drop the roped rock he used as an anchor, and they could lie down in the boat, under the thwarts; it would be a little awkward, but what did that matter? The boat would rock gently on the waves, and they would feel the warmth of the rising sun on their naked skin.

But perhaps they would be wiser to unfurl the sail and put more distance between themselves and the town before they risked a halt. He wanted to be well away by full day. It would be difficult to resist temptation with her so close, looking at him and smiling happily. But it was more important to secure their future.

When they got to their new home they would say they were already married, they had decided. Until now they had never spent a night in bed. From today they would eat supper together every evening, and lie in each other's arms all night, and smile knowingly at one another in the morning.

He saw a glimmer of light on the horizon. Dawn was about to break. She would be here at any moment.

He felt sad only when he thought about his family. He could happily live without his brothers, who still treated him as a foolish kid and tried to pretend that he had not grown up smarter than both of them. But he would miss Pa, who all his life had told him things he would never forget, such as: 'No matter how well you scarf two planks together, the joint is always the weakest part.' And the thought of leaving Ma brought tears to his eyes. She was a strong woman. When things went wrong, she did not waste time bemoaning her fate, but set about putting matters right. Three years ago, Pa had fallen sick with a fever and almost died, and Ma had taken charge of the yard – telling the three boys what to do, collecting debts, making sure customers did not cancel orders – until Pa had recovered. She was a leader, and not just of the family. Pa was one of the twelve elders of Combe, but it was Ma who had led the townspeople in protest when Wigelm, the thane, had tried to increase everyone's rents.

The thought of leaving would have been unbearable but for the joyous prospect of a future full of Sunni.

In the faint light Edgar saw something odd out on the water. He had good eyesight and he was used to making out ships at a distance, distinguishing the shape of a hull from that of a high wave or a low cloud, but now he was not sure what he was looking at. He strained to hear any distant sound, but all he picked up was the noise of the waves on the beach right in front of him.

After a few heartbeats he seemed to see the head of a monster, and he suffered a chill of dread. Against the faint glow in the sky he thought he saw pointed ears, great jaws and a long neck.

A moment later he realized he was looking at something even worse than a monster: it was a Viking ship, with a dragon head at the tip of its long, curved prow.

Another came into view, then a third, then a fourth. Their sails were taut with the quickening south-westerly breeze, and the light vessels were moving fast through the waves. Edgar sprang to his feet.

The Vikings were thieves, rapists and murderers. They attacked along the coast and up rivers. They set fire to towns, stole everything they could carry, and murdered everyone except young men and women, whom they captured to sell as slaves.

Edgar hesitated a moment longer.

He could see ten ships now. That meant at least five hundred Vikings.

Were these definitely Viking ships? Other builders

had adopted their innovations and copied their designs, as Edgar himself had. But he could tell the difference: there was a coiled menace in the Scandinavian vessels that no imitators had achieved.

Anyway, who else would be approaching in such numbers at dawn? No, there was no doubt.

Hell was coming to Combe.

He had to warn Sunni. If he could get to her in time, they might yet escape.

Guiltily he realized his first thought had been of her, rather than of his family. He must alert them, too. But they were on the far side of the town. He would find Sunni first.

He turned and ran along the beach, peering at the path ahead for half-hidden obstacles. After a minute he stopped and looked out at the bay. He was horrified to see how fast the Vikings had moved. There were already blazing torches moving swiftly, some reflected in the moving sea, others evidently being carried across the sand. They were landing already!

But they were silent. He could still hear the monks praying, all oblivious of their fate. He should warn them, too. But he could not warn everyone.

Or perhaps he could. Looking at the tower of the monks' church silhouetted against the lightening sky, he saw a way to warn Sunni, his family, the monks and the whole town.

He swerved towards the monastery. A low fence loomed up out of the dark and he leaped over it without slowing his pace. Landing on the far side, he stumbled, regained his balance and ran on.

He came to the church door and glanced back. The monastery was on a slight rise, and he could view the whole town and the bay. Hundreds of Vikings were splashing through the shallows on to the beach and into the town. He saw the crisp, summer-dry straw of a thatched roof burst into flames, then another, and another. He knew all the houses in town and their owners but, in the dim light, he could not figure out which was which, and he wondered grimly whether his own home was alight.

He threw open the church door. The nave was lit by restless candlelight. The monks' chant became ragged as some of them saw him running to the base of the tower. He saw the dangling rope, seized it and pulled down. To his dismay, the bell made no sound.

One of the monks broke away from the group and strode towards him. The shaved top of his head was surrounded by white curls, and Edgar recognized Prior Ulfric. 'Get out of here, you foolish boy,' the prior said indignantly.

Edgar could hardly trouble himself with explanations. 'I have to ring the bell!' he said frantically. 'What's wrong with it?'

The service had broken down and all the monks were now watching. A second man approached: the kitchener, Maerwynn, a younger man, not as pompous as Ulfric. 'What's going on, Edgar?' he said.

'The Vikings are here!' Edgar cried. He pulled again at the rope. He had never before tried to ring a church bell, and its weight surprised him.

'Oh, no!' cried Prior Ulfric. His expression changed from censorious to scared. 'God spare us!'

Maerwynn said: 'Are you sure, Edgar?'

'I saw them from the beach!'

Maerwynn ran to the door and looked out. He came back white-faced. 'It's true,' he said.

Ulfric screamed: 'Run, everyone!'

'Wait!' said Maerwynn. 'Edgar, keep pulling the

rope. It takes a few tugs to get going. Lift your feet and hang on. Everyone else, we have a few minutes before they get here. Pick something up before you run: first the reliquaries with the remains of the saints, then the jewelled ornaments and the books – and then run to the woods.'

Holding the rope, Edgar lifted his body off the floor, and a moment later he heard the boom of the great bell sound out.

Ulric snatched up a silver cross and dashed out, and the other monks began to follow, some calmly collecting precious objects, others yelling and panicking.

The bell began to swing and it rang repeatedly. Edgar pulled the rope frenziedly, using the weight of his body. He wanted everyone to know right away that this was not merely a summons to sleeping monks but an alarm call to the whole town.

After a minute, he felt sure he had done enough. He left the rope swinging and dashed out of the church.

The acrid smell of burning thatch pricked his nostrils: the brisk breeze was spreading the flames with dreadful speed. At the same time, daylight was brightening. In the town, people were running out of their houses clutching babies and children and whatever else was precious to them: tools and chickens and leather bags of coins. The fastest were already crossing the fields towards the woods. Some would escape, Edgar thought, thanks to that bell.

He went against the flow, dodging his friends and neighbours, heading for Sunni's house. He saw the baker, who would have been at his oven early: now he was running from his house with a sack of flour on his back. The alehouse called the Sailors was still quiet, its occupants slow to rise even after the alarm. Wyn the jeweller went by on his horse, with a chest strapped to his back; the horse was charging in a panic and he had his arms around its neck, holding on desperately. A slave called Griff went by carrying an old woman, his owner. Edgar scanned every face that passed him, just in case Sunni was among them, but he did not see her.

Then he met the Vikings.

The vanguard of the force was a dozen big men and two terrifying-looking women, all in leather jerkins, armed with spears and axes. They were not wearing helmets, Edgar saw, and as fear rose in his throat like vomit he realized they did not need much protection from the feeble townspeople. Some were already carrying booty: a sword with a jewelled hilt, clearly meant for display rather than battle; a money bag; a fur robe; a costly saddle with harness mounts in gilded bronze. One led a white horse that Edgar recognized as belonging to the owner of a herring ship; one had a girl over his shoulder, but Edgar saw gratefully that it was not Sunni.

He backed away, but the Vikings came on, and he could not flee because he had to find Sunni.

A few brave townsmen resisted. Their backs were to Edgar so he could not tell who they were. Some used axes and daggers, one a bow and arrows. For several heartbeats Edgar just stared, paralysed by the sight of sharp blades cutting into human flesh, the sound of wounded men howling like animals in pain, the smell of a town on fire. The only violence he had ever seen consisted of fistfights between aggressive boys or drunk men. This was new: gushing blood and spilling guts and screams of agony and terror. He was frozen with fear.

The traders and fishermen of Combe were no match for these attackers whose livelihood was violence. The locals were cut down in moments, and the Vikings advanced, more coming up behind the leaders.

Edgar recovered his senses and dodged behind a house. He had to get away from the Vikings, but he was not too scared to remember Sunni.

The attackers were moving along the main street, pursuing the townspeople who were fleeing along the same road; but there were no Vikings behind the houses. Each home had about half an acre of land: most people had apple trees and a vegetable garden, and the wealthier ones a hen house or a pigsty. Edgar ran from one backyard to the next, making for Sunni's place.

Sunni and Cyneric lived in a house like any other except for the dairy, a lean-to extension built of cob – a mixture of sand, stones, clay and straw – with a roof of thin stone tiles, all meant to keep the place cool. The building stood on the edge of a small field where the cows were pastured.

Edgar reached the house, flung open the door and dashed in.

He saw Cyneric on the floor: a short, heavy man with black hair. The rushes around him were soaked with blood and he lay perfectly still. A gaping wound between his neck and shoulder was no longer bleeding, and Edgar had no doubt he was dead.

Sunni's brown-and-white dog, Brindle, stood in the corner, trembling and panting as dogs do when terrified.

But where was she?

At the back of the house was a doorway that led to the dairy. The door stood open, and as Edgar moved towards it he heard Sunni cry out.

He stepped into the dairy. He saw the back of a tall Viking with yellow hair. Some kind of struggle was going on: a bucket of milk had spilled on the stone floor, and the long manger from which the cows fed had been knocked over.

A split second later Edgar saw that the Viking's opponent was Sunni. Her suntanned face was grim with rage, her mouth wide open showing white teeth, her dark hair flying. The Viking had an axe in one hand but was not using it. With the other hand he was trying to wrestle Sunni to the ground while she lashed out at him with a big kitchen knife. Clearly he wanted to capture her rather than kill her, for a healthy young woman made a high-value slave.

Neither of them saw Edgar.

Before Edgar could move, Sunni caught the Viking across the face with a slash of her knife, and he roared with pain as blood spurted from his gashed cheek. Infuriated, he dropped the axe, grabbed her by both shoulders and threw her to the ground. She fell heavily, and Edgar heard a sickening thud as her head hit the stone step on the threshold. To his horror she seemed to lose consciousness. The Viking dropped to one knee, reached into his jerkin and drew out a length of leather cord, evidently intending to tie her up.

With the slight turn of his head, he spotted Edgar.

His face registered alarm, and he reached for his dropped weapon, but he was too late. Edgar snatched up the axe a split second before the Viking could get his hand on it. It was a weapon very like the tool Edgar used to fell trees. He grasped the shaft with a familiar two-handed grip. In the dim back of his mind he noticed that handle and head were beautifully balanced. He stepped back, out of the Viking's reach. The man started to rise.

Edgar swung the axe in a big circle.

He took it back behind him, then lifted it over his head, and finally brought it down, fast and hard and accurately, in a perfect curve. The sharp blade landed precisely on top of the man's head. It sliced through hair, skin and skull, and cut deep, spilling brains.

To Edgar's horror the Viking did not immediately fall dead, but seemed for a moment to be struggling to remain standing; then the life went out of him like the light from a snuffed candle, and he fell to the ground in a bundle of slack limbs.

Edgar dropped the axe and knelt beside Sunni. Her eyes were open and staring. He murmured her name. 'Speak to me,' he said. He took her hand and lifted her arm. It was limp. He kissed her mouth and realized there was no breath. He felt her heart, just beneath the curve of the soft breast he adored. He kept his hand there, hoping desperately to feel a heartbeat, and he sobbed when he realized there was none. She was gone, and her heart would not beat again.

He stared unbelievingly for a long moment; then,

with boundless tenderness, he touched her eyelids with his fingertips – gently, as if fearing to hurt her – and closed her eyes.

Slowly he fell forward until his head rested on her chest, and his tears soaked into the brown wool of her homespun dress.

A moment later, he was filled with mad rage at the man who had taken her life. He jumped to his feet, seized the axe and began to hack at the Viking's dead face, smashing the forehead, slicing the eyes, splitting the chin.

The fit lasted only moments before he realized the gruesome hopelessness of what he was doing. When he stopped, he heard shouting outside in a language that was similar to the one he spoke, but not quite the same. That brought him back abruptly to the danger he was in. He might be about to die.

I don't care, I'll die, he thought; but that mood lasted only seconds. If he met another Viking, his own head might be split just like that of the man at his feet. Stricken with grief as he was, he could still feel terror at the thought of being hacked to death.

But what was he to do? He was afraid of being found

inside the dairy, with the corpse of his victim crying out for revenge; but if he went outside he would surely be captured and killed. He looked about him wildly: where could he hide? His eye fell on the overturned manger, a crude wooden construction. Upside down, its trough looked big enough to conceal him.

He lay on the stone floor and pulled it over him. As an afterthought he lifted the edge, grabbed the axe and pulled it under with him.

Some light came through the cracks between the planks of the manger. He lay still and listened. The wood muffled sound somewhat, but he could hear a lot of shouting and screaming outside. He waited in fear: at any moment a Viking could come in and be curious enough to look under the manger. If that happened, Edgar decided, he would try to kill the man instantly with the axe; but he would be at a serious disadvantage, lying on the ground with his enemy standing over him.

He heard a dog whine, and understood that Brindle must be standing beside the inverted manger. 'Go away,' he hissed. The sound of his voice only encouraged the dog, and she whined louder.

Edgar cursed, then lifted the edge of the trough, reached out and pulled the dog in with him. Brindle lay down and went silent.

Edgar waited, listening to the horrible sounds of slaughter and destruction.

Brindle began to lick the Viking's brains off the blade of the axe.